WHAT ARE MAMMALS?

Animal Book for 2nd Grade

Children's Animal Books

You may be familiar with some mammals such as horses, dolphins, and elephants, but there are many that you might not be so familiar with. In this book, you will learn about some of the different species of mammals.

WHAT ARE THE CHARACTERISTICS OF A MAMMAL?

Mammals are a certain class of animals. There are several things that make an animal a mammal:

- ➮ They have to have glands to provide milk in order to feed their young.
- ➮ They are warm-blooded.
- ➮ They have hair or fur.

Lion

Humans are mammals as well as dogs, horses and whales. Most of them have teeth, other than the anteater which does not have teeth.

WHERE CAN THEY BE FOUND?

Mammals can be found in all types of environments including on land, underground and in the ocean. Some, like bats, have the ability to fly.

Bat

Dolphins

THREE TYPES OF MAMMALS

Often, they are separated into three different types based on how they give birth and how they care for their young.

LIVE YOUNG

Most of them give birth to live young instead of laying eggs similar to reptiles or birds. These mammals are referred to as placental mammals.

Red Fox

MARSUPIALS

The mammals that carry their young in a pouch are known as marsupials. Examples of marsupials are the koala, the opossum and the kangaroo.

EGG LAYING

There are a few mammals that lay eggs and they are known as monotremes. Monotremes include the long-nosed spiny anteater and the platypus.

Platypus

Blue Whale

THE LARGEST MAMMAL

The Blue Whale is the biggest mammal. It resides in the ocean and can be more than 80 feet long. The elephant is the largest land mammal which is followed by the rhinoceros and the hippopotamus (which spends quite a bit of time in the water).

The Kitty's hog-nosed bat is the smallest mammal at only 1.2 inches long and weighing less than ½ pound. It is also known as the bumblebee bat.

Piglets

ARE THEY INTELLIGENT?

Mammals have distinctive brains and often are quite intelligent. The most intelligent mammals are humans. Some of the other mammals that are intelligent are the elephant, the chimpanzee, the dolphin, as well as the pig. Yes, pigs are considered to be one of the most intelligent animals!

WHAT DO THEY LIKE TO EAT?

Mammals are carnivores, which means they like eating meat. Carnivores include tigers, seals, lions, and the polar bear, which is the largest carnivore mammal. There are also mammals that eat only plants and they are known as herbivores. Giraffes, cows, and elephants are a few of the herbivores. Mammals that enjoy eating both plants and meat are known as omnivores. Humans are known as omnivores.

Tiger

Blue Whale

BLUE WHALES

By far, the blue whales are the largest animals around the world. Even the largest dinosaur doesn't even come close to its size.

IT'S A MAMMAL?

The blue whale is referred to as a species of mammal known as a cetacean and is related to the baleen whale. Balaenoptera muscolus is its scientific name. They reside in each of the oceans around the world. They migrate to the tropics for breeding and giving birth and they feed in higher latitudes.

Krill in the sea

WHAT DO THEY EAT?

Blue whales have to filter their food through their bony, stiff, comb-like teeth known as baleen plates. Their typical diet consists of krill and copepods. They can eat as much as 8,000 pounds of krill each day during their peak consumption time period. It's estimated that it takes about 2,200 pounds of food to fill its stomach.

HOW BIG ARE THEY?

Blue whales are just enormous. Its heart is about the size of a small car and can pump 10 tons of blood through its body. The aorta of the blue whale is so large that a human could crawl through it. They have been reported to grow to lengths of 110 feet in the Antarctic, but typically they grow to be between 80 and 90 feet long and weigh more than 200 tons. The females are typically bigger than the males, and the blue whales of the northern hemisphere are usually smaller than the ones in the southern hemisphere. They are a light bluish gray on their dorsal side and a mottled whitish gray on their bellies. Some may have a yellowish belly.

BABY BLUE WHALES

The baby blue whale is referred to as a calf. When they are born, they are about the size of an elephant and they start growing very quickly. It gains about 200 pounds a day and will be about 50 feet long when it is six months old. The calf will live from its mother's milk for its first six months and by then its baleen plates have grown so that it can eat the krill.

WHAT NOISES DO THEY MAKE?

In addition to being the largest mammal on the planet, it also is the loudest. It is unknown why they sing, but they sing very loudly. Typically, a blue whale call may last for 10 to 30 seconds and it is a very low frequency between 10 and 40 Hz. To put this in perspective, as humans, you can probably only hear down to about 20 Hz, so you probably won't even be able to notice this "loud" whale call.

Blue Whale in Indian Ocean

ARE THEY CONSIDERED TO BE ENDANGERED?

The population of the blue whale worldwide is unknown; however, they are considered as endangered according to the United States Endangered Species Act. It is believed that the population is currently between 5,000 and 12,000. For many years, they were hunted exclusively for their large quantities of meat, baleen and blubber. While the blue whales are protected, the population of the blue whales do not show much sign of recovery.

RED KANGAROO

The largest of the kangaroos is the red kangaroo. You will find them throughout most of Australia and they are the biggest mammal living in Australia. Macropus rufus is its scientific name.

Red Kangaroo

Red Kangaroo

HOW BIG DOES THE RED KANGAROO GET?

The male red kangaroo is much larger than the female of the species, growing almost 10 feet long and weighing about 200 pounds. The females grow to be less than 4 feet long and about 80 pounds. The males will typically stand about 5 feet tall, but some of them have grown to be about 6 feet tall.

Red Kangaroo mob

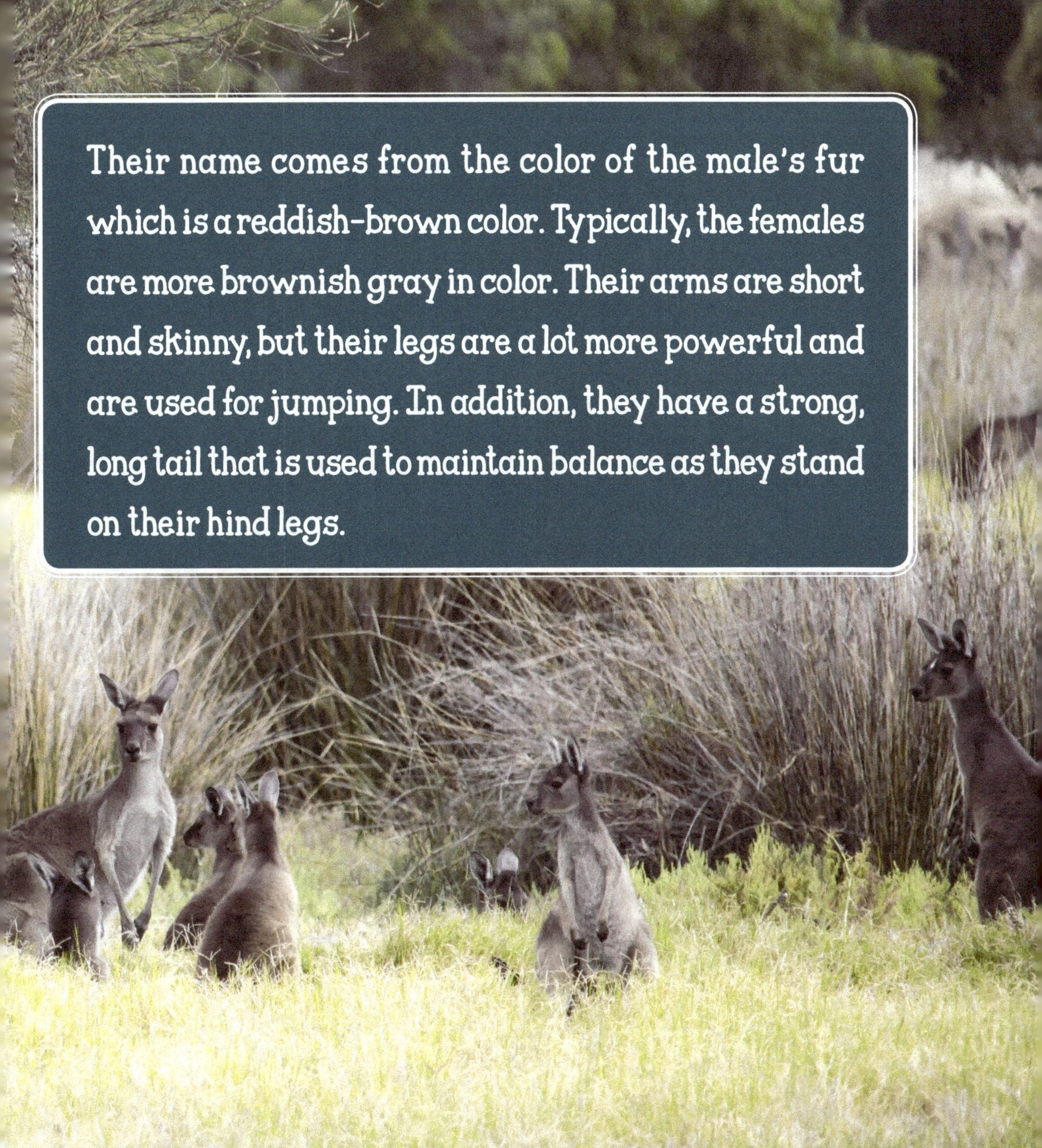

Their name comes from the color of the male's fur which is a reddish-brown color. Typically, the females are more brownish gray in color. Their arms are short and skinny, but their legs are a lot more powerful and are used for jumping. In addition, they have a strong, long tail that is used to maintain balance as they stand on their hind legs.

HOW FAR CAN THEY JUMP?

The male of the species has the ability to jump 30 feet with only one jump. In addition, they use this ability to quickly travel as fast as 30 miles an hour.

WHAT DO THEY EAT?

They are herbivores, and graze mostly on grasses. Since they reside in areas that are mostly arid and dry, they can go for long periods of time without water.

Wallaby

WHAT IS A MARSUPIAL?

The type of animal that gives birth to its baby very early is known as a marsupial. Once the baby is born, it lives in its mother's pouch as it continues to develop. The kangaroo is a marsupial. The babies are referred to as joeys and are very tiny, being only about an inch long when they are born. They will live in their mother's pouch for approximately eight months after they are born.

DO THEY ACTUALLY BOX?

Occasionally, the males will fight and it looks as though they are boxing. At first, they will push one another with their forearms. If the fight proceeds to get serious, they start kicking each other with their strong legs. The use their tail for support as they deliver these strong kicks.

Kangaroos fighting

Platypus

THE PLATYPUS

Sometimes referred to as the duck-billed platypus, its scientific name is Ornithorhynchus anatinus. It can be found in eastern Australia, and is a semiaquatic egg-laying mammal, which makes it a monotreme.

WHAT DO THEY EAT?

The platypus is known as a carnivore an it eats insect larvae, annelid worms, and freshwater yabby which it digs out from the riverbed using its snout or catches it while swimming. It has cheek-pouches which it uses for carrying its prey to the surface. It has to eat about 20% of its weight every day for survival which means that it has to spend about 12 hours each day in search of food.

DANGERS OF THE PLATYPUS

Its unusual appearance baffled European naturalists once they first encountered it, and some thought of it as a hoax. There is a spur on the hind foot of the male platypus that is able to deliver a venom that can cause severe pain to humans.

IS IT PROTECTED?

The platypus had been hunted for its fur until the early 20th century, when it became a protected species. It is not under an immediate threat even though there has only been limited success with captive breeding programs as well as being vulnerable to the effects of pollution.

For additional on these mammals and many others you
can go to your local library, research the internet, and
ask questions of your teachers, family and friends.

Visit
BABY PROFESSOR
EDUCATION KIDS
www.BabyProfessorBooks.com
to download Free Baby Professor eBooks
and view our catalog of new and exciting
Children's Books